THE
COLOUR
OF ASIA

THE COLOUR OF ASIA

Published by:
FormAsia Books Limited
706, Yu Yuet Lai Building
45, Wyndham Street
Central, Hong Kong
www.formasiabooks.com

Published 2003
ISBN 962-7283-65-7
Text and photographs © FormAsia Books Limited

Written by Peter Moss
Art Direction by Hans Lindberg
Digital Artwork by Carmela Escasa
FormAsia Marketing by Eliza Lee
Printed in Hong Kong
Printed by Sing Cheong Printing Company Limited
Film separations by Sky Art Graphic Co., Limited

Source of photographs:
Pages 30/31 Hoa-Qui: Imagechina
Pages 88/89,92/93 Magnum: Paris
All remaining images: FormAsia Books Archives.
Photographic Assistant Sathish Gobinath

THE
COLOUR
OF ASIA

Peter Moss

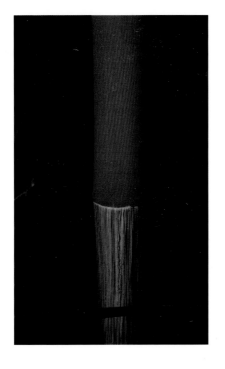

FormAsia

Warmer Colours for Hotter Climates

Colour, that visual attribute which objects transmit through the harmonics of refracted light, seems more varied in Asia than it does elsewhere in the world. Perhaps because the light is stronger, more intense, more revealing.

"In what distant deeps or skies burnt the fire of thine eyes?" asked William Blake, in his poem *Tiger, Tiger, Burning Bright*. His question summarised the wonder of early Europeans venturing into the farther regions of Asia.

What seemed the most alien and exotic to their cautiously restrained sensibilities generally had to do with the unexpected extravagance of the colours they encountered. Their weather had filtered their sunlight to the more subtle, pastel shades. Were they available in that age, they would have been in urgent need of sunglasses. Colours bombarded their senses.

In tropical Asia even the *flora* is more florid; the foliage more aggressively green, the blossoms more blatantly effulgent. And, with his tiger left to blaze in the forests of the night, what would Blake have had to say about the rest of the *fauna*; the birds of a myriad hues, the beetles of pyrotechnic profusion?

Studies have indicated that those who live in climates with a lot of sunlight prefer warm bright colours; while those from climates with less sunlight favour cooler, less saturated colors.

The Bride Wears Red

It would come as a shock to her guests if a bride in Europe or the United States chose a crimson wedding gown, but at a traditional Chinese wedding ceremony it would provoke comment if she did not. To Western eyes, red connotes anger, whereas in China it connotes festivity and good fortune.

During China's Cultural Revolution, the more extreme Red Guards wanted to change all the traffic lights. They saw it as an insult to have red as the stop sign when to them it connoted progress, strength and victory. So assertive is Chinese red that is has been adopted into the artist's catalogue as a colour in its own right. In the words of a colour coordinator, "While a maroon has more blue, and tomato red more orange, Chinese red is simply one thing – red!"

The West associates yellow with caution, even cowardice. The East associates it with honour and royalty. In the language of Shakespeare, green can imply sexual arousal, immaturity or even jealousy. In the Orient it suggests youth and growth, while jealousy is described by the Chinese as "red eye disease". White indicates purity and virtue in Western eyes, whereas in much of the East it is the colour of mourning and humility.

Colour, then, is ethnically and culturally oriented. It can have more to do with ritual and etiquette than with skin tone. And the varieties of ethnicity and culture in Asia make this area of the world an artist's palette of boundless diversity.

Like a Deep Ocean, or Eternal Sky

Such an abundance of colour can sometimes astonish fellow Asians travelling to other parts of their continent. Visiting mosques in Malaysia, Yano Hidetake, a researcher at the Institute of Japanese Culture and Classics of Kokugakuin University, was *"awed by the architectural details and their blue theme."*

"While I had seen religious architecture from a number of religions before," remarked Hidetake, *"this was the first time I had directly observed any based on the colour blue. The colour was like a deep ocean or eternal sky, expressing a depth removed from the sacred space of the religious facility, and into which the land (this world) blended. Merely standing there and viewing that colour was enough to give one a sense of freshness and revival."*

When the seasons shift, and the light is diluted, the colours of Asia become more subtle, dissolving into mists and mystery as vagrant clouds cling to mountain peaks, as shade upon shade of ever paler blue recede to infinities of distance.

Festive Colours

More than any other
human activity, festivity
is associated with colour,
and seldom to more
stridently visible effect
than in Asia, where
colour reigns paramount.
Some Asian festivals
are entirely based upon
colour, the most notable
example being the
festival of *Holi*, with
which Indians mark
the advent of spring
and the death of the
demoness *Holika*.

Holi, and its celebrants,
are no respecters of
persons. When venturing
outdoors you would be
well advised to wear
your most disposable
clothing. Never deficient
in colour, even in
their most mundane
circumstance, the lives of
ordinary Indians become
veritably steeped in it on
this multi-hued day, when
ordinary street scenes
are transformed into
aquatints, submerged

below water so that the colours run.

If *Holi* ranks high among India's favourite festivals, *Ganesh*, the elephant-headed son of *Shiva*, looms large among its most popular deities. Regarding him as "The Lord of Obstacles" Hindus beseech *Ganesh* to remove impediments from their path, aware that he is equally capable of placing them there should they fail in their obeisances to his jovially benign and ubiquitous presence.

Understandably then, elephants have an especially revered place in festivals that call for the full panoply of pomp and circumstance. Elaborately caparisoned in richly embroidered cloths, these behemoths tread majestically along corridors of celebrants, who pave their way with prayers and petals.

Nowhere is the revered pachyderm processed with greater magnificence and solemnity than in Sri Lanka, where as many as a hundred or more elephants play a pivotal role in the *Esala Perahera* celebrations.

The *Esala Perahera* festival dates back to the arrival, from India, of the sacred tooth relic of *Lord Buddha*. According to ancient chronicles, Sri Lanka's King Kirthisiri Meghawanna, who reigned in Anuradhapura from 300-331 AD, made elaborate arrangements to receive and enshrine the relic in Kandy's sacred Temple of the Tooth. The King also decreed that the relic be taken around the city once a year, a ritual that has since been faithfully observed throughout history.

Although elephants enjoyed equally

gargantuan status in the ritual observances of Burma, Thailand, Cambodia and other South East Asian kingdoms, they never achieved quite the same impact in China. While acknowledged as an auspicious animal, and accorded a place among the stone menageries lining the routes to imperial tombs, the Chinese elephant ranked nowhere near as high in public esteem as the dragon, whose heraldic supremacy in the Chinese zodiac has never been challenged.

The lack of living examples has allowed the Chinese to loose their unbridled imaginations upon this most favoured of mythological beasts. The greater the size, the greater the efficacy of the imperial emblem. For especially august Chinese festivals it is not uncommon to see dragons of a hundred

feet or more rippling their sinuous, silk-encased forms like rivers of gold through streets lined with delighted bystanders. While the appearance of the creature is made to seem as alarming as possible, every Chinese child knows that its ferocious aspect conceals a benevolent disposition; a truth further verified by the presence of a lone masked dancer, leading the dragon on with a paper ball at the end of a wand, symbolising the pearl of wisdom which the dragon forever yearns to grasp.

The glowering red visage of the dragon also serves as figurehead for the slim racing vessels built to compete in the annual dragon boat races, which in Hong Kong have long commanded international entries. And red of an equally clamorous hue is the

predominant colour of the flags and pennants bedecking the spectator stands for this much loved and eagerly supported event.

Red being the colour most feared by demons and malevolent beings, Chinese New Year is greeted with every nuance of that tone from cerise and carmine to scarlet and crimson. Attendant upon all Chinese festivals, from the feast of the hungry ghosts to viewing of the mid-autumn moon with ingeniously fashioned lanterns of every shade, shape and size, colour reaches the fullness of its symbolic significance with the Lunar New Year festivities.

Shifting Vapours

Together with the fabric that gave this fabled route its name, the Silk Road carried and popularised the trade in incense, long before Gaspar, of the Three Wise Men, bore frankincense from southern Arabia to the Bethlehem manger where Jesus was born.

Like a lamp burning in darkness, the aroma of incense permeates the senses, lightens the intellect and imparts, to even the most mundane of experience, an air of the extraordinary. Added to the olfactory sensations, its visible appearance, layering the atmosphere in bands of blue and grey, suggests the intangible and mysterious, the shifting vapours that dissolve the boundaries between the known and the unknown.

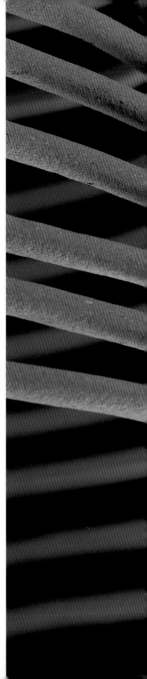

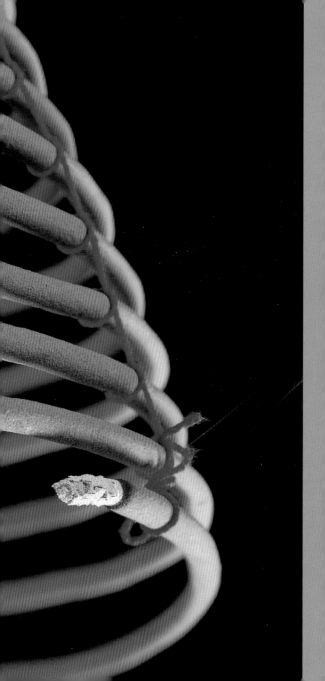

An undated Chinese poem, written in memoriam, associated incense with loss:

I breathe in the cool incense from the metal brazier, while thinking about a poem for my dear friend Lu Wa. My sandalwood-hearted companion spits out plum blossoms of smoke, looking like the cloudy fog of the other world. Perhaps it is the soul of my friend the old mountain man in the vapour's dense patterns?

No wonder that, since pre-Egyptian times, incense has been associated with ritual and priestly observance, most especially in man's ceaseless efforts to commune with the spirit world.

As aid to elevated consciousness, and accompaniment to religious ceremonials,

27

it has not lost its links
with the metaphysical.
Swinging censers still
accompany the
processionals of many
assorted faiths. Bowls
of smouldering incense
stand at the entrance
to the typical Japanese
shrine, to be wafted into
the faces of arriving
worshippers, while
elegant coils that
prolong their combustion
for hours, if not days,
hang from the smoke-
blackened rafters of
Chinese temples.

In some cultures the
lighting of incense is
viewed as an end in
itself, taking the place
of candles burning at
Christian altars. It serves
as an offering, symbolic
of prayers ascending to
the heavens. One widely
held Chinese belief
regards incense as
a channel for
communication –
a "telephone" line
connecting man with the
divine. The "call" to the
other world begins as

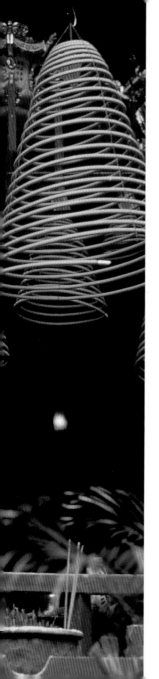

the incense is lit and ends once the stick is consumed.

The lighting of incense to accompany the presentation of food offerings is seen not as part and parcel of the gift, but rather as a signal inviting the recipient gods to partake of the sacrificial feast.

Such communications are governed by time-honoured protocols. While most Chinese gods might be summoned with vermilion-tipped incense, vegetarian divinities may require yellow sticks, while other spirits are liable to demand green ones. Thais light three sticks to pay homage to the *Buddha*, but only one when honouring their ancestors. The rules vary from culture to culture, and between rituals, depending on whether these are devotional, celebratory, placatory or festive.

The Way of the Brush

The fundamental component of Chinese calligraphy, as with painting, is the line – and the best calligrapher, along with the true artist, is identified by his ability to maintain the long, flowing contours of a single brush stroke to capture the essence of his subject.

Other brush strokes may be appended later, but the connoisseur will look for that core, that backbone which commenced the undertaking, and from which all else followed.

Because of this common feature, the two arts – painting and calligraphy – shared, from their very beginnings in earliest times, a close mutual relationship.

The written language of China itself evolved from

ideograms; simplified pictorial representations of the objects described, which then developed into increasingly abstract patterns over the centuries.

Hence the close relationship between poetry and painting, so that often a poem will complement the pictorial subject on the same scroll. Scholar-statesmen were in the vanguard of this melding, a leading exponent being the Sung Emperor Hui-tsung (1082-1135). He used poetry to test painters on their ability to express, with ink and paper, the enchanted world conjured up in the written word.

Escape Routes

Hui-tsung followed the trend, established two centuries earlier during the T'ang dynasty (618-907), that favoured

landscape and flower-and-bird paintings as the supreme forms of pictorial arts.

The Chinese saw paintings of mountains, forests, fields and gardens as much-needed respite from the cares and travails of daily existence. Such diversions were the next best thing to opting out, wandering off and becoming footloose vagrants living on wild fruits, mountain air and large doses of stupendously grandiloquent natural scenery.

If they stood, long contemplating a panoramic scroll so large that it might spread over an entire wall, it was because the view portrayed had the ability to transport them away from the vexations of the material world into a peaceful, carefree realm. The way of the brush became their means of escape.

All the Tea in China

Tea, the first letter in "Tranquility", found its greatest champion in Lu Yu who, during the mid-T'ang dynasty, returned from seclusion as a Buddhist monk to summarize the knowledge and experience of his predecessors and contemporaries in the first world's first compendium on the arts of tea, the great *Tea Classic* (Ch'a Ching). Certainly all the tea in China would have been, even then, sufficiently varied and provincially distinctive to merit such a compilation.

Among other things, this prodigious work dispensed important pharmaceutical knowledge:

Tea is of the cold nature and may be used in cases of blockage or

stoppage of the bowels. He who is generally moderate, but is feeling hot or warm, given to melancholia, suffering from aching of the brain, smarting of the eyes, troubling of the four limbs, or affliction in the hundred joints, may take tea four or five times. Its liquor is like the sweetest dew of Heaven.

Spared our contemporary prohibitions on false claims in advertising, Lu Yu's classic spread like the allegedly beneficial effects of the plant itself through the body corporate of China. It instituted the art of tea drinking across the entire sub-continent, making avid tea drinkers of everyone from emperor and minister to farmer and merchant. And, looking to China for their cultural lead, the neighbouring countries of Korea, Japan, and Southeast Asia were quick to follow suit.

The Heavenly Grain

Over much of tropical Asia, the sun is mirrored in a patchwork quilt of inundated rice fields, framed and filigreed by delicate strands of elevated bund just wide enough for the passage of farmers walking single file.

Jewelled clusters of palm and bamboo, with occasional banana groves and fruit orchards, form the grace notes to a panorama that can otherwise confuse the eye with its half terrestrial, half celestial prospects.

Viewed from above, as we fly over seemingly endless vistas of iridescent jade, it would appear that the earth has devised giant nets with which to snare an inverted firmament. Was this, we wonder, the sight that inspired the

invention of the solar heating panel? For surely long exposure to unclouded sunlight will raise the temperature of those shallow pools? Effectively we appear to be looking at a giant natural incubator, whose captured heat is required to force the growth of a grain vital to the nourishment of an increasingly abundant populace.

So essential is this staple commodity that *"Without rice, even the cleverest housewife cannot cook,"* chaff the Chinese, *"Rice chokes when eaten in haste"*, caution the Koreans and *"A meal without rice is no meal at all,"* jest the Japanese. Some of the earliest missionaries in the Orient translated a key passage in the Lord's Prayer into *"give us this day our daily rice".*

Nowhere is the intricacy and ingenuity of repetitive patterns of rice

field more evident than
in those areas where
the terrain rises and the
cultivations ascend in
ever-narrowing, terraced
contours, storming
impossible heights.
Often the higher the
climb, the richer the soil,
especially in large areas
of Java, Bali, the
Philippines and Japan.
For on the upper flanks
of still festering
volcanoes lie the richest
loams, encouraging
farmers to risk disturbing
unquiet gods with the
blades of buffalo-
drawn ploughs.

Hence the prolific
festivals, throughout
this earthquake-prone
region, to placate the
divinities that govern
the seasons and
soothe the sleep of
subterranean giants.

Reverence for rice found
its earliest expression
in India, where its
cultivation originated
some ten thousand years
ago. South Indians call

rice *anna Lakshmi, anna* meaning "food" and *Lakshmi* being the Goddess of prosperity. *Dhanya Lakshmi* is generally depicted clasping sheaves of rice to her ample bosom.

The worldwide custom of throwing rice at newlyweds can also be traced to South India, where raw rice, mixed with *kumkum* to redden it, is known as *mangala akshadai* and showered over the bridal pair.

But the rituals of rice are not restricted to India. The Angkabau of Sumatra use special rice plants to denote the Rice Mother, *Indoea Padi*. The people of Indochina treat ripened rice in bloom as if it were a pregnant woman, capturing its spirit in a basket. The earliest rice growers of the Malay Peninsula often looked upon the wife of the cultivator as a pregnant woman for the first three

days after their harvest was stored.

Among the Cantonese of southern China, the words for rice and food are identical. "Have you eaten rice?" is substituted for the "How are you?" employed as a common form of greeting in the West. In Thailand, the family is summoned to the table with the call "Eat rice."

The Toradja tribes of Indonesia consider rice to be of heavenly origin. So hallowed is the seed that it is taboo to plant any other crop in their paddy fields. What better augury than that the heavens should see themselves reflected in the lakes whence spring the tender green shoots of their infant grain?

Calamitous Vice Masquerading as Cultural Virtue

Described in the early nineteenth century by Thomas de Quincey as "portable ecstasies" that "might be had corked up in a pint bottle", opium has acquired a chequered history. Lauded for years as laudanum, in which opium derivatives were consumed in a mixture of alcohol, it was prescribed as "a panacea for all human woes". However it fell seriously into disrepute when probing alchemists of narcotic extremism transformed it into a source of more ultimate oblivion. But viewed from a standpoint that – admittedly with difficulty – can overlook its perniciously addictive traits, together with its villainous role in the annals of imperialism and its notoriety as the foundation for lucrative

drug empires and warlords, opium remains an intrinsically colourful commodity.

This colour derived not just from the literary vein of de Quincey's *"Confessions of an Opium-Eater"* but from its metamorphosis as it followed its rainbow-hued journey from poppy to opium pipe. Reds, blacks and intermediary umber were the predominant tints of this spectrum, travelling down the light scale from the brilliant scarlets of poppy petals nodding in the harvest fields. Here the white latex dripped from incised poppy pods to congeal, darken and oxidize overnight, for collection in the morning in its raw form as a thick, pasty substance varying from brown to black.

Following the traditional opium trail, sombre grey pack trains transported the crop to its illicit

destinations, which ended in the exotic paraphernalia of the opium dens. Far from being necessarily dark and dingy, these haunts of the addicted were often festively decorated and lavishly furnished, the trappings themselves raising and embellishing the opium habit to great heights of pretension, under which the calamitous vice masqueraded almost as a cultural virtue.

Yet the seductive lure could not entirely disguise the baneful consequence. The poet Keats, whose heart ached, while a drowsy numbness pained his sense, "as though of hemlock I had drunk, or emptied some dull opiate to the drains", was rescued, in the nick of time, only by the song of a nightingale.

No Paradise but Bali

Bali is the quintessential
island. Outside
Denpasar stands a statue
commemorating the ritual
suicide of men, women
and children who in
1904 walked into the
cannonades of weeping
Dutch invaders vainly
appealing for
their surrender.

Bali's simultaneous
acceptance of western
incursions and rejection
of western mores is
the consequence of
a remarkably potent
faith, which permeates
all communal life
and provides the
enduring foundation
to everything Balinese.

The people who have
held this rock steadfast
against the stream of
history derived their
vigorous spiritual beliefs
from the Hinduism
imported by Indian
traders, long before

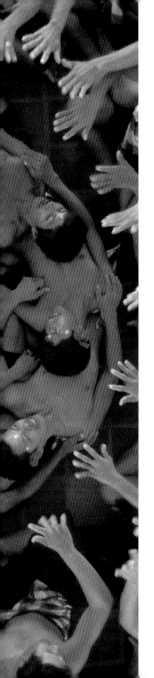

neighbouring Java surrendered to the inroads of Islam. But while those beliefs are rooted in recognisable Hindu theology, they have evolved into inimitably Balinese styles that accord their pantheon of divinities an appearance entirely their own.

Highly expressive of the inward-concentrated, self-contemplative character of this unique people is the *ketjak* dance, whose participants, representing the simian hosts of monkey lord *Hanuman*, form a circle facing the narrator at their core, who relates crucial chapters from the Hindu epic of the *Ramayana*.

The Balinese idea of paradise is to be reborn in another, equally heavenly Bali – without the tourists. They have no dreams of a Valhalla or any state of existence but

that to which they remain so devoted.

True hell, for a Balinese, would be a reincarnation condemned to colour blindness. For no landscape is more drenched in colour than the landscape of Bali.

"Without colour I could not see," murmured an artist of lyrically beautiful renditions of that landscape, crowded with incident and suffused in polychromatic diversity.

No people in Asia are more fecund in their creativity. Every village has its artisans and weavers, its wood carvers and painters, its poets and storytellers, its dancers and musicians. And every village appears to find some compelling reason to celebrate one or other festival for every week of the calendar.

Such celebrations lavish fresh daubs of paint upon an already saturated canvas, producing a flow of colours that scroll past the eye in seemingly endless procession.

Here lies an island apart, yet ever on the move, a permanent pageant deployed across a luminous landscape. Women wend their way to temples with votive offerings mountainously heaped upon their heads, *gamelan* orchestras, loud with gong and cymbal, parade to the next *Barong* dance, chanting priests lead palanquins of the dead to their ritual cremations.

Bali is so busy that it really hasn't noticed history passing by. Least of all does it care to catch up with it.

The Versatile Tree

The colour saffron comes from the jakfruit tree (*artocarpus integrifolius*) whose cambium layer is a brilliant, orange-yellow, sticky wood, the sap of which is a natural adhesive. This resin can be boiled into a thick glue that enables carpenters to dispense with nails and dowels. But the jakfruit tree is principally regarded as the source of a dye which, since the dawn of their faith, Buddhist monks have adopted as their chosen colour.

The essential simplicity and uniformity of the robe that identifies a Buddhist monk derives from a long tradition of self-denial and abstemious withdrawal from indulgence and temptation. Even before the birth of Buddhism, in the 6th century BC, Hindu ascetics were

wandering India in the barest of clothing, sometimes salvaged from decayed corpses in burial grounds.

Such remnants were sewn together into a rough cape, using thread made from the fibrous spine of the coconut frond. The effect was akin to wearing sandpaper; the objective to give notice that all desires of the flesh had been abandoned, that the body was valueless, that mind and spirit were all.

However *Lord Buddha*, when he devised his Path of the Middle Way, taught his disciples to shed worldly possessions but not necessarily their skins. Hence the compromise of the saffron robe, whose varying shades can be so subtle as to denote the particular monastery to which its wearer is attached.

Today, in addition to the ubiquitous saffron which everyone associates with Buddhism, there is a ruddy shade of brown used mainly by monks who have withdrawn so completely from the world that they are seldom seen. In Cambodia and Thailand, widows who have retired into nunneries adopt an all-white garb.

The Serene Countenance

Carried along the trade currents of the Silk Road, the seeds of Buddhism took root throughout Asia, propagating offshoots in ever expanding territories from its original heartland in India to Afghanistan, where the Taliban recently shocked the civilised world by destroying some of its earliest monuments, and onward via Turkistan,

Mongolia and China
to Japan. Other routes
took it to Sri Lanka,
Burma, Thailand,
Indo-China and the
archipelago now
known as Indonesia.

Along these
omnidirectional courses
it inspired an astonishing
range of iconic
representations of its
founder, varying from
lean and austere to
sturdy and rotund.
All of these nonetheless
share the one common
characteristic of a
serenity that transcends
the mundane and
imparts to this, of
all faiths, a sublime
enigma that begs
comprehension.

The Panoply of Faith

As was the case in Mediaeval Europe, the earliest architecture of Asia found its ultimate and most sublime expression in religion. Whether mosque, pagoda, shrine or temple, the Asian place of worship is instantly recognisable, not only for the creed it serves but for the geographical region in which it is located.

As the longest surviving Asian doctrine, Hinduism can lay claim to some of the oldest examples of religious architecture, many of them colossal in stature, towering over sprawling acres of temple complex. And more than any other faith – more even than Buddhism which was to follow its lead – the typical Hindu temple is encrusted with statuary and bas reliefs, testifying

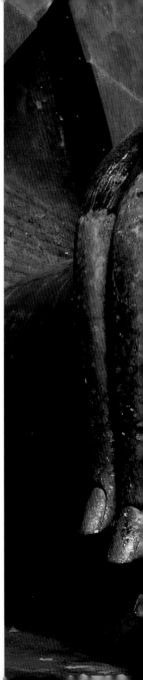

to the intricate pantheon of deities it celebrates.

While superficially resembling the Hindu model in this regard, Buddhist examples employed their carved panels and embossments to portray the lives of Buddha and his acolytes, much as Europe's early Christian churches used theirs to illustrate the lives of Christ and his disciples.

Hindu traders took their faith with them when they established mercantile communities in Indo-China, Malaysia and the islands now embraced within Indonesia, where only Bali endures as a healthy offspring of that gentle colonisation.

Elsewhere in South East Asia – most notably in Malaysia and Singapore – Hindu temples are of more recent provenance; largely the products of immigrants from South

India, imported during the British colonial era when plantations were expanding faster than the local labour force could supply the necessary workers.

Monumental Ruins

Following on the heels of Hinduism, as another import from the Indian sub-continent, Buddhism made wider and more lasting inroads, producing what would eventually include some of the world's most monumental ruins.

Among the latter, Borobudur, in Java, and Angkor, in Cambodia, are indisputably the best known and most romantic, having been buried and left to marinate for centuries in the jungle. Nothing so stimulates the imagination as the rediscovered evidence of lost civilizations.

Ironically, while Buddhism survived in most of the countries to which it travelled, including Sri Lanka, Tibet, Myanmar, Thailand, much of the former Indo-China, China and Japan, it withered in its country of origin, where Hinduism adopted some of its precepts and set out to demonstrate that the rest was superfluous.

Proselytizing Priests

Next in the order of arrivals came Islam, introduced by Arabic traders who taught that all that had preceded them was profoundly ungodly and unfit for preservation. Hence the disappearance of Hinduism and Buddhism from most of Indonesia – save Bali.

Last on the scene – but only just – came Christianity, brought in by Portuguese explorers and the proselytizing priests who accompanied them. Unfortunately for them, their advent was just a shade too historically late to win much ground in the longer established religious strongholds.

In southern Japan, for example, St. Francis Xavier wandered with Anger in search of converts, Anger being not only the condition to which he was occasionally reduced through his frustrations, but also the name of one of the few Japanese he managed to win over to his faith.

Thanks to their Spanish colonisation, the Philippines provided much more fertile ground for missionary zeal, and it was here that a titanic struggle commenced between the two

religions that had, from the outset, marched with a sword in one hand and a sacred scripture in the other.

ℛeligious Leapfrog

The battle lines in the geography of Asian religions have been nowhere more clearly defined than in the southern Philippines, where Christianity and Islam set out to play leapfrog through these outer isles of Asia.

On April 8, 1521 Ferdinand Magellan arrived in Cebu and – ignoring the evidence of occupation provided by thousands of inhabitants – "discovered" the island for the Europeans who were to follow. He planted a cross and picked a fight with the local chieftain, Lapu-

lapu, that led to the now legendary Battle of Mactan.

Magellan was killed in one of the most stunning reversals the Spaniards had yet encountered in their bloody conquests of new worlds, but forty-four years later, in February 1565, Spain sent another expedition, headed by Miguel Lopez de Legaspi, which eventually succeeded in colonizing Cebu and the central islands of the Visayas as well as the northern islands of Luzon.

By the seventeenth century, the hot volcanic flow and counter-flow of volatile and sometimes incendiary beliefs had largely congealed into sedimentary bedrock, and the religious topography of Asia has been essentially stratified ever since.

Waking the Tiger

If Nature designed the tiger's stripes for camouflage, why did the evolutionary process select such an arresting combination of colours? Why did Blake's "immortal hand or eye" frame such "fearful symmetry"?

Little wonder that in Asia the tiger came to symbolise great power, while its imitators were, in the words of China's Chairman Mao Zedong, dismissed as mere "paper tigers".

He had more cautionary things to say about the genuine article. "In waking a tiger," he advised, "use a long stick". For in China as much as elsewhere in Asia, no animal had come to symbolize, more effectively, the essential colours of ferocity. There too the tiger's strident black and yellow stripes were seen as a walking billboard of *Noli Me Tangere* or "*Touch Me Not*".

From coast to coast across southern India's Malabar to Coromandel, no character was to prove more feared and revered than the great Tippoo Sultan, Tiger of Mysore. In his seventeen years as ruler of that coveted state, from 1782 to 1799, he cleverly played one intruding colonial power against another, employing French officers to train his army in its resistance to British inroads.

Had he not been such a dedicated Anglophobe, Tippoo might have endeared himself to those seeking to deprive him of his kingdom, for the British love of heroes extends even to their enemies. But he really went too far by ordering the construction of a life-

sized wooden model of a tiger mauling a prostrate British redcoat. This mechanical contraption incorporated an organ worked by a pair of bellows, which forced air through the soldier's mouth to emit a whistling wail of helplessness.

*T*iger, Tiger, Burning Out

It was left to playwright George Bernard Shaw to point out that "When a man wants to murder a tiger he calls it sport; when a tiger wants to murder him he calls it ferocity." In Shaw's day men so frequently hunted the tiger for sport, usually on the backs of elephants and in the company of maharajahs, that the animal was quickly decimated. Had he lived long enough, Blake might have revised his poem to read "Tiger, tiger, burning out".

While pursuing and harassing it almost to extinction, the British revered the tiger as the embodiment of courage and employed it as an emblem of Empire, most especially befitting the Jewel in their Crown, Imperial India.

Their reverence found its apogee in the death of a particular tiger on the plains outside Jamalpur, in Bihar. There the beast in question was found embracing, in death, the body of its assailant, who had made somewhat of a hash of trying to shoot it.

So enchanted were the romantically inclined discoverers of this heroic death struggle that they commanded two identical marble tombs to be erected side by side at the very scene of battle; one for the tiger and one for its adversary.

Beauty in the Eye of the Moment

There is no art more affecting than the transient; the beauty savoured in the knowledge that it must soon vanish or decay. The remains of a day, swept into the last effulgence of a sunset, the bloom on a flower about to fade, the first smile on the face of an infant which no photograph or video image will ever fully recall. It's the qualities of the ephemeral and the irrecoverable that set the seal on the moment; the reminder that only here, only now, can we enjoy what we are seeing. They endow the experience with a sad wistfulness that each spring causes thousands of Japanese revellers to sigh with wonder under boughs laden with cherry blossom.

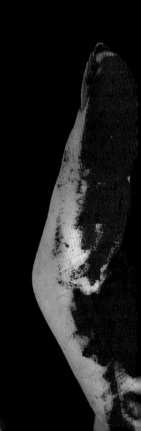

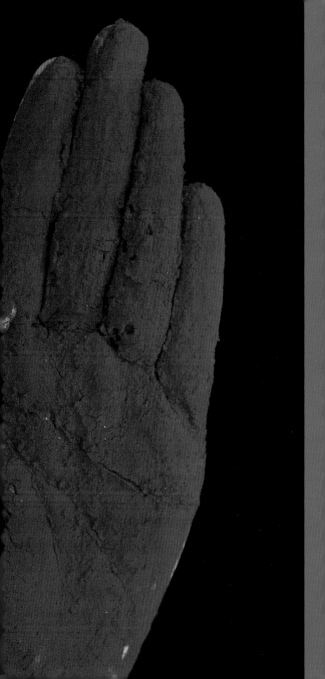

To fully experience art you must accept its frailty and its imminent loss.

Henna is just such an art form. Derived from the Persian name for *Lawsonia inermis*, a bushy, flowering tree originally found in Asia, Australia and along the Mediterranean coasts of Africa, henna has been used for at least five millennia to decorate the hands and feet.

Among early Egyptians it was considered ill-mannered not to dye the fingernails a reddish hue with henna. Traces of henna have been found on the hands of Egyptian mummies up to five thousand years old.

Henna ceremonial painting assumes an element of sanctity among many diverse cultures in India, Africa, and the Middle East. The Indian name for henna is *mehndi*, as is

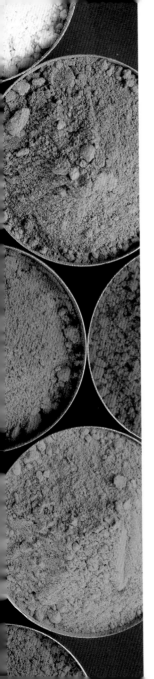

the name of the body art associated with its use. Intricate designs are painted as part of the marriage ceremony. Lord Shiva's wife, Parvati, decorated herself with henna to charm a husband difficult to please.

The styles of *mehndi* vary from region to region, their intrinsic symbolism evolving over generations to imply different meanings to different cultures. Whereas Arabic designs are generally large floral patterns on the hands and feet, Indians traditionally employ fine, thin lines for more delicate paisley effects, sometimes covering entire hands, forearms, feet and shins.

The popularity of henna has grown rather than diminished over the years, perhaps because it is perceived as a form of temporary tattooing for the timid and indecisive. In western cities it is now possible to find specialist beauty parlours offering henna painting as an added feminine glamorization.

But other uses are also being explored for the plant that gave the human body its least enduring embellishment. The Indian Journal of Pharmacology recently published a paper on *The Effect of Lawsonia Inermis on Memory And Behaviour Mediated Via Monoamine Neurotransmitters.*

Possibly we may some day derive, from the very same source, both the gratification of a short-lived pleasure and the means to recapture its essence in a fully restored recollection. And then some indefinable dimension that added to our enjoyment will itself be gone.

The Third Eye

The area of the human forehead above and between the eyebrows is considered by Hindus to be the seat of the intellect. It is the vanishing point of concentration into which yogis retire when they meditate to become one with Brahman. Here lies the precise location of the spiritual third eye, the *dibya-drishti*, or Eye of Knowledge, throne of the *antar-guru*, or the "teacher inside".

The two visible eyes are receivers, observing the physical dimensions of the world. The invisible third eye is the perceiver – the inner sight – the vision that bears witness to the truth of past, present and future.

The Hindu *Upanishads* describe a human being as a city with ten gates. Nine gates (eyes, nostrils, ears, mouth,

urethra and anus) lead to the outside world. The tenth gate, the third eye, opens onto the inner worlds: the whole spectrum of levels of human consciousness.

It is important therefore to ensure that this focal point, this concealed camera lens into the power of the intellect, remains at all times cool and unfevered, so as to assist maximum concentration.

Hence the *tilaka*, the distinguishing hallmark of the Hindu, compounded of sandalwood paste or some other cooling substance, applied to this spot to reduce its temperature and elevate its composure so that the wearer remains of stable mind and thought.

The Hindus are not alone in their respect for the third eye. In Buddhist art, the third eye is figured as a gem on the forehead of *Buddha*.

But only Hindu believers wear the *tilaka* as badge of their faith.

For the lay worshipper, the most common *tilaka* is the one applied after the performance of a ritual *puja* or *arati*, where the sandalwood paste is dyed vermilion. But over the course of time, the *tilaka* has also come to indicate sectarian distinctions. Devotees of *Shiva* inscribe three horizontal lines of sacred ash on their foreheads, to remind themselves of the God's threefold nature in creation, preservation and destruction.

Followers of *Vishnu* apply three vertical lines of sandalwood to denote *Vishnu's* powers of protection, while those who follow *Devi (Shakti)* apply a round or slightly elongated red mark to evoke the supreme power of *Adi Parashakti*, the Universal Mother.

A Landscape Punctuated by Turbans

The aridity of Rajasthan, which sprawls over an abundance of desert, cries out for colour much as its sparse vegetation yearns for water. Which is doubtless why dwellers of that monotone landscape stand out so stridently from their barren backgrounds.

Here is one province of India where both men and women make equal claim on the full spectrum of the rainbow in their choice of attire. Elsewhere on the sub-continent masculine embellishment is generally more restrained, whereas Rajasthani men impinge upon the unpractised eye with the emphasis of multi-hued exclamation marks, topped by turbans. Encountering a fraternity

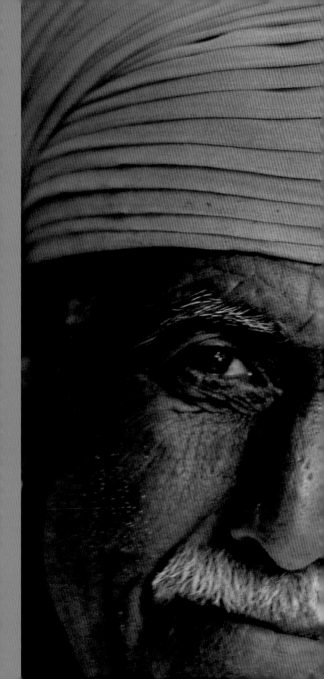

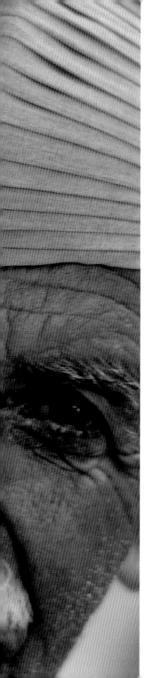

of them en masse is the visual equivalent of drowning in hyperbole.

In Rajasthan it would be the ultimate in bad taste for a man to appear in public without his turban. And this essential topknot has to be both of respectable length and correctly wound. A turban is variously called a *pagari*, *pencha*, *sela*, or *safa*, depending upon its size and style. A *pagari*, for example, is wound from material usually 82 feet long and eight inches wide, while a *safa* is shorter but also considerably broader, traditionally running to 30 feet in length and four feet in width.

Turbans being a gender definitive hallmark of Rajasthan, each region has its own distinctive way of tying this headdress. Urban turbans for formal events understandably require more care and attention

than is demanded of
more rustic raiment.
But whatever way you
wind it, mastering
different styles with just
a length of material
requires great skill.

Specialists in this art,
known as *pagribands*,
were employed by the
Rajas of Rajasthan and
others of the royal courts,
but less regal Rajasthanis
have generally taken
pride in practicing and
perfecting the art of
turban-tying themselves.

The selection of colours
is less a matter of
random whim than of
tribal identity, social
status, profession and
general place in the
community. It can also
be influenced by the
seasons. Those who
can afford to do so
wear different designs
and colours, depending
upon the calendar
and the occasion.
For example:

- *lahariya* turbans (from the Sanskrit word *lahara* meaning wave) are worn during the rainy season
- red and white *falguniya* turbans are donned in the spring
- pink, red, and green patterns signal festive events
- dull colors, such as dark blue, maroon or khaki, accompany more sombre circumstances, and
- the dotted *chunri* pattern signifies a birth in the family

Courtship requires special care in the choice of colour and the rakish angle at which the entire assemblage sits upon the brow, all of which has something in common with the amorous displays of the peacock. Little wonder that Rajasthan boasts more than sixty per cent of the entire Indian population of this decorative avian species.

The Invisible River and the Unwavering Pilgrims

In July 2002 the Jodhpur based Remote Sensing Service Centre of the Indian Space Research Organization announced that it had traced, with the aid of remote sensing satellites, the buried contours of India's mythical river, bearing the name of the Flowering One, the Hindu goddess *Saraswati*.

Mentioned in the *Rig Veda* and other ancient literature, this Himalayan-born watercourse is believed to have once flowed, parallel to the river Indus, through what is now desert before falling into the Arabian Sea.

Published accounts maintain that cataclysmic events in the Himalayas caused the Saraswati to disappear somewhere between 5000 and 3000 BC. Its loss deprived an immense tract of the Indian plains of its water supply, and led to climatic changes that transformed a formerly lush and green Rajasthan into an agricultural empty quarter.

The announcement of the invisible river's rediscovery has revived hopes of finding drinking water under the hot sands of the Thar desert. But while its resurrection may have profound implications for the populace of Rajasthan, it is unlikely to dampen the fervour of the millions of pilgrims who converge, each *Kumbh Mela*, at its legendary confluence with the rivers Ganga and Yamuna.

Here, at latitude 25.28 N and longitude 81.52 E, on the far reaching expanse of Uttar Pradesh,

is located the global epicentre of pilgrimage, focus of the largest recorded gatherings of humanity anywhere on the face of the earth. And here stands Allahabad, city of philosophy and learning, science and poetry subjected, every twelve years, to invasions that strain its logistical resources to the limits of endurance.

Visiting Allahabad in 1894, the American humorist Mark Twain was moved by the sight of "pilgrims plodding for months through heat to get here, worn, poor and hungry, but sustained by unwavering faith".

The single objective of these multitudes is to bathe in the sacred waters where the winged Garuda, in his flight to the gods bearing their elixir of eternity, accidentally spilled some of the contents of the pitcher, known as the *kumbh*. The word mela denotes a gathering, so that the combination of the two describes what has long been accepted as the most hallowed festival of the Hindu calendar.

Once the prescribed bathing days of the *Kumbh Mela* are past, and the millions of worshippers are dispersed, Allahabad can return to its sedate and respectable normality. Not so Varanasi, once known as Benares, where normality is a constant, year-round subjection to endless retinues of pilgrims who may not make it to the *Kumbh Mela* but who know that here too the river Ganga takes on an especially divine significance.

Varanasi is not so much a city that has grown as one that has accumulated, as if the sanctified waters have

deposited accretions of it over the centuries. Its older spires and pillars lean across the currents like venerable trees contemplating their stately demise. But when they crumble into the stream others will take their place, assembled more by whim than by design.

Here the word "colour", as an outward token of appearance or form, proves suddenly inadequate. Here there really is an insufficiency of adjectives to describe what neither the unpractised eye can amply absorb nor the inexperienced intellect fully comprehend. Varanasi is a destination of the spirit more than the mind, the transit point where the ethereal intersects with and transcends the corporeal. To its crowded strand come believers seeking rebirth, and those on the point of death, whose cremated ashes will be cast on the waters of eternity.

*M*oons, Melons and Minarets

The Mughal Empire, which swept into India with Zahiruddin Babar's conquest of Delhi in 1526, employed the graphic arts as the visual equivalent of the glorious verses of the Iranian poet Omar Khayyam. Equally inspired by Persian miniature paintings, they introduced their own variant in the distinctive Mughal style.

As with many a Chinese scroll, a typical Mughal miniature incorporates a phrase or a poem, usually written in Urdu script. The decorative look of this script merges into the painting and forms an essential component of the scene.

Within the microcosm of the Persian form, the artist added new themes, colours and stylistic departures.

Court scenes were frequently elevated to rooftops and set amid domes and minarets.

There regents and their paramours are seen regarding each other with eyes lustrously dark and longing, indicating appetites libidinously inclined, clearly not to be appeased by the viands, fruits and goblets they are sharing.

Prominent amid the repast will be suggestive indicators of what is to follow; a sliced melon, a burst pomegranate, a deflowered lotus. Overhead a moon will retreat into partial concealment behind a veil-like cloud, but remain nevertheless adequately placed to observe eventualities.

The background is usually taken up with hilly landscapes, where errant deer seem arrested in premonition of impending

159

consummation. Pigeons, ducks and herons wheel overhead, either taking flight or flocking to a scene fraught with as yet unspecified possibilities.

A Palpable Restraint

The effort at restraint is palpable. The artist, who would often be of the Hindu rather than the Muslim faith, is clearly exercising immense self-discipline to keep the captured moment comely and fitting for public display in a court of distinction, by a princely patron of the arts who must serve as the very model of decorum.

But the artist's own antecedents will have taken in such superb, yet shamelessly erotic works of art as the great Temple of Khajurao, whose candid and seemingly endlessly enterprising delineations

of the pursuit of love are scarcely suitable for a Mughal palace.

How to hint at fulfilment without portraying the climax? If there was ever an art form that supplies the answer to that conundrum, it lies in the art of the Mughal miniature. Patterns of love transmuted into floral arrangements, the implied symbolism of bird and beast and – above all – the steadfast gaze of the two principal protagonists as they raise clusters of grapes or freshly filled cups to lips that yearn to be elsewhere.

Although they might indulge such whims in private, commissioning sequels that portrayed the aftermath, when passion in the end proved altogether too compelling, Mughal emperors were on the whole more poetically inclined.

*L*ove on a Grander Scale

They preferred their expressions of love embodied in grander things; perhaps even in immense and ennobling works of architecture, such as the Taj Mahal. Shah Jehan ordered this masterpiece built as a memorial to his beloved wife, Mumtaz Mahal.

Aware he might be troubled by his relatives from the moment he took the throne from his own father, Jehangir, Shah Jehan had his brothers killed but neglected to kill his sons. One of them, Aurangzeb, rebelled against him in 1657 and imprisoned him in the octagonal tower of the Agra Fort.

That the world's greatest monument to love should have been made inaccessible to its creator, who spent his last years gazing at the

distant wonder of the Taj through barred windows from across the river, will remain one of the more refined cruelties of history.

Had he lived that long, Omar Khayyam might have committed this dilemma to one of his haunting verses. Although his full name was Ghiyath al-Din Abu'l-Fath Umar ibn Ibrahim Al-Nisaburi al-Khayyami, Omar Khayyam was his adopted abbreviation.

The name implies he was the son of a tent maker, and Khayyam played on this meaning when he wrote what has struck some as his own obituary:-
Khayyam, who stitched the tents of science, has fallen in grief's furnace and been burned. The shears of Fate have cut the tent ropes of his life, and the broker of Hope has sold him for nothing!